11+ English

WORKBOOK 1

Technical English Technique

Dr Stephen C Curran
with Katrina MacKay
Edited by Andrea Richardson

R_C__T

This book belongs to

Accelerated Education Publications Ltd

Contents

1. Classification   Pages
1. Odd One Out   3-7
2. Synonyms   8-12
3. Antonyms   12-18
4. Homonyms   18-23

2. Cloze
1. Multiple-choice - Type 1   24-34
2. Multiple-choice - Type 2   35-42
3. Word Bank   43-49
4. Missing Letters   49-58

3. Revision
1. Classification   59-60
2. Cloze   60-62

Chapter One
CLASSIFICATION

Classification involves first determining the meaning of a term or word and this process is called **semantics**. Once we have understood the meanings of the words or terms we can divide them up or separate them into their correct groupings according to type. When we group things by type and assign them a group name we call it **taxonomy**. This applies to any form of grouping, including animate and inanimate objects, word definitions, ideas and subject areas.

For example:
A simple taxonomy of vertebrates would be:
- mammals have hair or fur (cat, dog, horse)
- reptiles have scales (alligator, snake, turtle)
- birds have feathers and wings (eagle, sparrow, hummingbird)
- amphibians live on land and in water (frogs, toads, newts)
- fish breathe underwater using gills (shark, salmon, trout)

All work surrounding semantics and classification requires excellent spelling and vocabulary skills. Working through the Spelling & Vocabulary and Semantics workbooks will further develop these skills.

The following question types involve classification:

Odd One Out • **Synonyms** • **Antonyms** • **Homonyms**

1. Odd One Out

Odd One Out involves finding the word that does not belong to the group. This is achieved by establishing what the particular grouping is and which word does not fit into this grouping. There are a number of different types of odd one out question:

Noun Grouping • **Word Play** • **Word Meanings**

Example: Identify the word that does not fit into the group.
contemplate   ponder   act   cogitate   muse

1. Try and establish what the grouping might be. This may be difficult as you might not know the meanings of all the words. Most of these words appear to be about the process of thinking.
Contemplate, **ponder**, **cogitate** and **muse** all mean to think about something deeply or carefully.

2. Look for the word that does not fit into this particular classification. To **act** means to do something or to take action. This must be the odd one out as to take action is to do something rather than just think about it.

The odd one out is: act

a. Noun Grouping

This type of odd one out question focuses on identifying the particular **Noun Grouping**, e.g. oboe, flute, piccolo, clarinet, cor anglais and bassoon are all wind instruments.

Exercise 1: 1 Underline the odd one out:

1) beret   fez   bowler   visor   sombrero
2) tsunami   flood   hurricane   torrent   deluge
3) Kenya   Istanbul   Germany   Vietnam   Chile
4) cousin   aunty   mother   niece   sister
5) puma   gazelle   tiger   cougar   jaguar
6) lark   jackdaw   chaffinch   jay   dragonfly
7) veal   pheasant   duck   quail   turkey
8) Indian   Europe   Arctic   Atlantic   Pacific
9) colony   pack   pride   herd   group
10) popular   birch   elm   beech   willow

Record scores out of ten here ↓

Score

b. Word Play

This type of odd one out question focuses on the structural differences between words. It includes the following types:
- Matching Letters – a group of words that contain the same letters or combinations of letters, e.g. flee<u>ing</u> and buy<u>ing</u>
- Palindromes – words that read the same forwards and backwards, e.g. madam
- Rhyming Words – words that have the same sound or end with the same sound, e.g. note and boat
- Silent Letters – words that contain letters that are not sounded phonetically, e.g. dum<u>b</u> and <u>g</u>naw
- Semordnilaps – words that will spell another word backwards, e.g. tip spells pit backwards and vice versa

© 2014 Stephen Curran

Exercise 1: 2   Underline the odd one out:

1) drive   dragon   drink   demon   drone
2) rotor   tight   level   civic   kayak
3) below   crow   mound   go   although
4) trail   knife   bomb   receipt   echo
5) draw   trap   evil   moor   game
6) blue   shoe   queue   draw   screw
7) abridge   carnage   average   image   voyage
8) gnash   knave   gnome   knelt   gangue
9) lever   smart   later   straw   parts
10) refer   yummy   noon   did   radar

c. Word Meanings

This type of odd one out question focuses on spotting the meaning connection between a group of words, which identifies them as synonyms.
E.g. Funny: humorous, comical, hilarious, hysterical

Exercise 1: 3   Underline the odd one out:

1) gloomy   ecstatic   blissful   cheery   pleased
2) weak   vigorous   fragile   delicate   frail
3) novel   innovative   ancient   original   pioneering

4) beautiful   stunning   handsome   attractive   mediocre

5) irate   invalid   infuriated   incensed   irritated

6) abyss   poorly   ailing   infirm   unwell

7) catastrophe   disaster   triumph   calamity   debacle

8) maximise   augment   amplify   curtail   enlarge

9) soothe   pacify   provoke   lull   appease

10) dissuade   persuade   convince   sway   coax

d. Mixed Examples

Exercise 1: 4   Underline the odd one out:

1) stroll   meander   march   scamper   repose

2) joke   oak   yolk   baulk   soak

3) stream   tributary   lagoon   brook   rivulet

4) enthral   captivate   fascinate   squander   engross

5) moccasins   stockings   socks   tights   legwarmers

6) affable   hostile   pleasant   amenable   agreeable

7) bream   anemone   bass   mullet   haddock

8) chaos   archives   abscess   technique   orchid

9) rotator   eye   solos   sees   riser

10) grief   sorrow   ire   anguish   woe

Score

2. Synonyms

A **Synonym** is a word or phrase that means exactly or nearly the same as another word or phrase in the same language. Synonym questions are of two types:

Select the Synonym • **Spell the Synonym**

a. Select the Synonym

Example: Which one of the following words is a synonym of the word pursue?

sprint   compete   route   hound   proceed

1. Try to establish in your mind the meaning of the key word **pursue**. Pursue means to follow someone or something in order to catch or attack it, or achieve or attain it.

2. Examine each word closely to see how many of them you know the meanings of and then compare their meanings with the meaning of the word pursue.
   - **sprint** means to run very fast over a short distance. This word does mean to move quickly but does not contain the idea of chasing something or someone.
   - **compete** means to strive to win something by defeating those that oppose you. This word implies there is an opponent to defeat but there is no sense of the opponent being chased.
   - **route** means a way taken to get from one place to another. This word implies a journey but no one is being chased.

- **proceed** means to begin a course of action. This word does not specify what kind of action so it does not refer to chasing someone.

3. Only **hound** remains. Hound means to harass, persecute or hunt relentlessly. This word compares well with the meaning of pursue, which is to chase something or someone.

4. Check if both words are the same part of speech by putting them into the same sentence.
    'The police pursue criminals.'
    'The police hound criminals.'
Both of these words work in this sentence.

The correct synonym is: hound

Exercise 1: 5

Underline the word which is a synonym of the word in bold:

Score

1) **brave**   valiant   strong   scared   unbeaten

2) **funny**   humerus   amusing   laugh   normal

3) **hysterical** tears   hyacinth   misguided   emotional

4) **situation**   location   proximity   area   capital

5) **shrewd**   petite   mean   smart   mouse   miserly

6) **callous**   rough   difficult   grating   tough   cruel

7) **flounder**   stream   struggle   sink   aim   guard

8) **insipid**   bland   sickly   bright   cold   unwell

9) **breach**	blockage	break	form	strike	begin
10) **report**	terms	print	journal	article	define

b. Spell the Synonym

Example: Complete the word on the right by filling in the missing letters. It is a synonym of the word on the left.

announce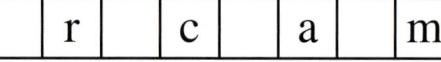

1. Focus on the completed word on the left and its meaning. To announce means to make something known publicly. This may give a clue to the word on the right.

2. Try out letters from the alphabet in one of the spaces. The most obvious space to try is the first one. The letter **r** can only follow certain letters in a word. Some of the likely possibilities would be **br**, **cr**, **dr**, **fr**, **gr**, **pr** and **tr**. This is a matter of trial and error.

b	r		c		a		m
c	r		c		a		m
d	r		c		a		m
f	r		c		a		m
g	r		c		a		m
p	r		c		a		m
t	r		c		a		m

3. There is likely to be a vowel after the first two letters and there are only five of these – **a**, **e**, **i**, **o** and **u**. Only **o** will work.

b	r	o	c		a		m
c	r	o	c		a		m
d	r	o	c		a		m
f	r	o	c		a		m
g	r	o	c		a		m
p	**r**	**o**	**c**		**a**		**m**
t	r	o	c		a		m

4. It is now fairly easy to spot the word, even without filling in more letters, as all the other possibilities do not spell proper words. The word proclaim does mean to announce or make something known publicly.

The correct synonym is: proclaim

Exercise 1: 6 Complete the word on the right by filling in the missing letters. It is a synonym of the word on the left:

1) **elegy** | | o | | m |

2) **erase** | d | | l | | | e |

3) **foul** | | | l | g | | r |

4) **elite** | e | | c | l | | | | v |

5) **govern** | m | | | | g | e |

6) **nag** | | a | d | g | |

7) **rascal** | s | c | | | d | | | l |

8) **caption** | | u | b | t | | t | | |

9) **loose** | u | | t | t | | c | | |

10) **habit** | c | | n | v | | t | | o |

Score

c. Mixed Examples

Exercise 1: 7 Complete or underline the word on the right that is a synonym of the word on the left:

1) **uniform**   shirt   even   unlikely   different   soldier

2) **kindle**   fire   douse   cherish   gentle   ignite

3) **reject**   discard   accept   destroy   endure   regress

4) **restrain**   give   free   confine   reserve   conscious

5) **imagine**   mundane   consider   know   envisage   mistake

6) **blend** | | | x |

7) **understanding** | c | | | p | | | h | | | | |

8) **libel** | s | l | | | d | | |

9) **mistake** | | r | | r | | r | |

10) **paternal** | | | | t | h | | l | |

Score

3. Antonyms

An **Antonym** is a word that has the opposite meaning to that of another word. Antonym questions are of two types:

Select the Antonym • **Spell the Antonym**

a. Select the Antonym

Example: Which one of the following words is an antonym of the word insult?

**offend   confer   compromise
complement   praise**

1. Try to establish in your mind the meaning of the key word **insult**. To insult means to act in an offensive or impolite way towards another person.

2. Examine each word closely to see how many of them you know the meanings of, and then compare their meanings with the meaning of the word insult.
   - **offend** means to cause someone to feel upset, annoyed or resentful and is a synonym of insult. However we are looking for an antonym.
   - **confer** means either to grant or award an honour to someone or to consult or have discussions with someone. This has nothing to do with being insulting.
   - **compromise** means to settle a dispute with both sides accepting some concessions (allowances are made by both parties). No insults are involved in this process.
   - A **complement** is a thing that is added to improve the quality of something else, e.g. salt complements food. It can also mean the number of persons or things that are required to make a group complete. This has nothing to do with the word insult. Do not confuse complement with the word compliment which means to congratulate or praise someone. If

compliment had been used it would be an antonym of insult.

3. Only **praise** remains. To praise means to express warm approval or admiration of something or someone. This is the opposite of insulting another and looks like the correct answer.

4. Check if both words are the same part of speech by putting them into the same sentence.
    'Your comments can insult someone.'
    'Your comments can praise someone.'
Both of these words work in this sentence.

The correct antonym is: praise

Exercise 1: 8

Underline the word which is an antonym of the word in bold:

Score

1) **juxtaposed**   distanced   long   close   associated

2) **naïve**   young   simple   experienced   taxing

3) **rude**   courteous   genuine   pliable   insolent

4) **absolute**   shoddy   unconfirmed   power   complete

5) **frenzied**   manic   calm   busy   hungry   panicked

6) **absent**   leave   missing   avert   vague   present

7) **expand**   enlarge   grow   dwindle   conserve   concise

8) **vitality**   energy   light   progress   lethargy   dinginess

9) **saintly**   wicked   pious   doubt   incorrect   godly

10) **boisterous**   nasty   verbose   loud   placid   playful

b. Spell the Antonym

Example: Complete the word on the right by filling in the missing letters. It is an antonym of the word on the left.

certainty | | a | | s | | h | o | | d |

1. Focus on the completed word on the left and its meaning. Certainty means the truth, a definite fact or reality. We now look on the right for a word that has the opposite meaning. This clue may give you the missing word straight away but, if not, proceed to the next step.

2. Try out letters from the alphabet in one of the spaces. The most obvious space to try is the first one. In this instance only a consonant will fit as no vowel will work. Most consonants are unsuitable and if you work through them some options would be **b, c, f, m** or **p** as possibilities. This is a matter of trial and error.

b	a	s	h	o	d
c	a	s	h	o	d
f	a	s	h	o	d
m	a	s	h	o	d
p	a	s	h	o	d

If this does not give you the word then move to the next step.

3. Try out letters from the alphabet in one other space where only a few letters could possibly fit. In the last part of the word there are limited letters that can work between the **o** and **d**. Only **o** will work as a vowel and **l** as a consonant.

	a		s		h	o	l	d
	a		s		h	o	**o**	d

4. **Hold** or **hood** must form the final syllable. If we use **hold** it is very hard to make a word that fits the meaning, as shown below.

b	a		s		h	o	l	d
c	a		s		h	o	l	d
f	a		s		h	o	l	d
m	a		s		h	o	l	d
p	a		s		h	o	l	d

5. The last syllable must be **hood** and the remaining letter combinations should be sufficient to identify the word, which is falsehood.

b	a		s		h	o	o	d
c	a		s		h	o	o	d
f	**a**	**l**	**s**	**e**	**h**	**o**	**o**	**d**
m	a		s		h	o	o	d
p	a		s		h	o	o	d

The correct antonym is: falsehood

Exercise 1: 9

Complete the word on the right by filling in the missing letters. It is an antonym of the word on the left:

1) **qualify** — f _ _ i _
2) **ominous** — h _ p _ f _ _
3) **candid** — u _ t _ r _ _ h _ f _ _
4) **huge** — _ _ i c r _ s _ _ _ _ c
5) **repulsive** — _ t t _ _ _ _ i _ v _
6) **alter** — r _ m _ i _
7) **renovate** — d _ m _ _ g _
8) **belligerent** — _ e _ a _ _ f _ _
9) **integrity** — _ i _ h o _ _ _ t y
10) **praise** — r _ p r _ _ _ n d

Score

c. Mixed Examples

Exercise 1: 10

Complete or underline the word on the right that is an antonym of the word on the left:

1) **weak** — feeble robust tired puny bulky
2) **fresh** — stagnant new pungent moist lively

3) **fierce**   brutal wild tender vicious restful

4) **shabby**   dilapidated rotten intricate elegant

5) **lessen**   growth surge complex fasten slacken

6) **clean** | p | | l | | | | d |

7) **separate** | c | | n | | c |

8) **integrate** | | i | v | | d | |

9) **attentive** | | x |

10) **evade** | c | | n | f | r | | t |

Score

4. Homonyms

Homonyms occur when two or more words have the same spelling or pronunciation but have different meanings.

Example: Which word will go equally well with both sets of words in the brackets?

(refuge, sanctuary)   (protect, safeguard)

asylum   guard   haven   lodge   shelter

At least one of these words is a homonym, which means it has more than one meaning and will match both sets of words in the brackets.

© 2014 Stephen Curran

1. Consider the meanings of the words in each set of brackets and establish the difference between them.

   (refuge, sanctuary)

   A **refuge** or a **sanctuary** is a noun and is a place that provides safety from pursuit, persecution, or other danger.

   (protect, safeguard)

   To **protect** or **safeguard** is a verb and means to keep someone or something safe from harm, injury, or damage.

2. Now check the meaning of each word in turn to see if it matches either of the sets of words in the brackets:
   - An **asylum** is a place where people stay who have fled from another country for political reasons. This is a place of safety but does not mean to protect or safeguard.
   - To **guard** is a verb that means to watch over, in order to protect or control, but does not mean a place of safety.
   - A **haven** is a noun and is a place of refuge and safety but does not mean to protect.
   - A **lodge** can be a noun that means a small house in the grounds of a large house, occupied by an employee. To lodge is also a verb that means to pay rent to live in a property. Neither of these meanings fit with the words in the brackets.
   - A **shelter** is a place of refuge or sanctuary and it also means to protect or safeguard. This is the correct answer as it embraces both meanings.

The correct homonym is: shelter

a. Level 1

Exercise 1: 11 Underline the one word which will link the two pairs of bracketed words:

1) (overcome, defeat)
   (hit, strike)

   drum   beat   bored   sleepy

2) (well, good)
   (charge, penalty)

   fine   bright   payment   polite

3) (fib, untruth)
   (recline, lounge)

   rest   chair   tale   lie

4) (bright, sunny)
   (weightless, airy)

   brilliant   clear   light   casual

5) (intend, propose)
   (nasty, unkind)

   cruel   mean   average   aim

6) (stem, stalk)
   (chest, case)

   box   flower   trunk   container

7) (healthy, fit)
   (pit, shaft)

   well   strong   ditch   hole

8) (guide, direct)
   (leash, chain)

   steer   rope   tether   lead

9) (breeze, gale)　　　twist　gust　wind　roam
　　(snake, meander)

10) (line, queue)　　　row　din　strip　fight
　　(dispute, argument)

Score

b. Level 2

Exercise 1: 12　Underline the one word which will link the two pairs of bracketed words:

1) (coiled, looped)　　　twist　wind　graze
　　(injury, lesion)　　　　wound　kink

2) (wilderness, wasteland)　delay　desert　discard
　　(abandon, leave)　　　　dessert　deposit

3) (beat, hammer)　　　strike　pulse　vibrate
　　(throb, pulsate)　　　ache　pound

4) (matter, substance)　glad　subject　content
　　(happy, satisfied)　　　issue　ready

5) (group, ensemble)　band　assembly　belt
　　(ring, loop)　　　　strap　collective

6) (crushed, minced)   terrain creased field
    (earth, soil)   ground milled

7) (chequered, plaid)   measure quota gauge
    (assess, inspect)   tartan check

8) (tolerate, endure)   stand bear stomach
    (carry, support)   hold allow

9) (underdone, bloody)   grisly rare scarce
    (unique, unusual)   frequent gory

10) (admirer, devotee)   supporter wave fan
     (cool, waft)   serene chill

Score

c. Level 3

Exercise 1: 13   Underline the one word which will link the two pairs of bracketed words:

1) (chorus, catchphrase)   refrain choir stop
   (abstain, cease)   reprise sing

2) (curtsy, stoop)   bob nod bow
   (arc, curve)   arch sag

3) (verge, shore)   edge collection hoard
   (store, stock)   margin bank

4) (shout, snap)   whisper bark murmur
   (howl, yap)   hiss utter

5) (lure, enticement)   insult provoke tempt
   (taunt, tease)   bait bribe

6) (forlorn, miserable) wild glum dismal
   (deserted, barren)   empty desolate

7) (obstruct, hinder)   block chunk deter
   (slab, wedge)   unit impede

8) (produced, yielded) slog gave created
   (tire, weary)   bore exhaust

9) (council, jury)   team beam board
   (plank, slat)   squad wood

10) (origin, source)   foundation root burrow
    (forage, delve)   basis dig

Score

Chapter Two
CLOZE

Cloze procedure involves supplying missing words or parts of words that have been deleted from a portion of text. Cloze tests require the ability to understand context and vocabulary in order to identify the correct words or parts of words that belong in the deleted passages of text.

Parts of Speech

It is important in cloze activity to understand the parts of speech, as this can often assist in identifying the missing words. The part of speech describes the function of the word in the sentence and not the word itself. Many words can function as different parts of speech depending on how they are used in a sentence.

For example:
David wanted to **train** (verb) to operate a locomotive so he could join a **train** (adjective) company and drive a **train** (noun) every day.

- Nouns – the name of a person, place or thing, e.g. spoon
- Adjective – a word that describes a noun, e.g. **soup** spoon
- Verb – a 'doing' word that indicates activity, e.g. ran
- Adverb – a word that describes a verb, e.g. ran **fast**
- Conjunction or Connective – a joining word that links two parts of a sentence, e.g. and or but

- Preposition – a word showing how words relate to each other. It can be thought of as indicating position, e.g. came **after** dinner
- Pronoun – a word that replaces a noun, e.g. he or them

Context

The context or meaning of the passage or sentence in which the missing word or word with missing letters is situated can offer clues to solving the cloze questions.

There are three types of cloze test:

Multiple-choice • **Word Bank** • **Missing Letters**

1. Multiple-choice - Type 1

In the first type of **Multiple-choice** style question there are three alternatives for each missing word in the cloze passage.

Example: Read the following cloze passage and identify the missing word from each multiple-choice option.

Global Warming

Global warming is the occurrence of increasing average air (**1.** rises, temperatures, illnesses) near the surface of the (**2.** Earth, Mars, plateau) over the past two centuries. Since the middle of the last century, climate scientists have collected detailed data of various (**3.** cloud, meteor, weather) patterns, which includes information on temperature and storm

> incidence and other possible influences on (**4.** growth, climate, plants) such as ocean (**5.** currents, waters, depth) and the chemical composition of the atmosphere.

1. Read the whole passage and try to establish what it is about, as this will provide clues for each missing word. This passage concerns the phenomenon of global warming, which means our planet is getting hotter due to human activity. The following approach applies to all five questions but this explanation focuses on questions 1 and 2:

   Global warming is the occurrence of increasing average air (**1.** rises, temperatures, illnesses) near the surface of the (**2.** earth, Mars, plateau) over the past two centuries.

2. Eliminate any words that do not fit grammatically.

   Global warming is the occurrence of increasing average air **rises** near the surface of the **Mars**.

   Neither **rises** nor **Mars** work in questions 1 and 2 as **rises** is a verb and is the wrong part of speech and **Mars** cannot have the, the definite article, preceding it in the sentence.

3. Check for any words that do not fit the meaning.

   Global warming is the occurrence of increasing average air **illnesses** near the surface of the **plateau**.

   Neither **illnesses** nor **plateau** work in questions 1 and 2 as **illnesses** have nothing to do with global warming and **plateau** is just a flat piece of ground and global warming involves the whole planet.

4. Try the remaining words in the sentence and see if they work.

Global warming is the occurrence of increasing average air **temperatures** near the surface of the **earth**.

Both these words work in the sentence. The answers are: **1. temperatures 2. Earth**

Using the same process, the other questions will give the following answers: **3. weather 4. climate 5. currents**

After each exercise has been completed and marked it is important to look up in a dictionary the meanings of the words that have been incorrectly selected. It is also crucial to take note of any grammatical, punctuation, syntactical or contextual errors that might have led to the wrong selection.

Exercise 2: 1

Underline the correct words to complete the sentences:

Score

1) The (veterinarian, pilot, magician) made a dove (dissipate, appear, conceal) out of (thick, thin, weightless) air.

2) Knitting is the (capacity, art, talent) of using (needles, sticks, pointers) to loop yarn to form a (cloth, stuff, wool).

3) The train was (late, deferred, delayed) for 20 minutes (due, because, for) to fallen leaves on the (track, road, train).

4) Mount Kilimanjaro is the (widest, highest, largest) mountain in Africa, (situated, left, contained) in Tanzania, the mountain is a (hidden, undeveloped, dormant) volcano.

5) The climbers were (defunct, lost, evaded) on the mountain and had fears of (frostbite, cold, chill) as the night (draw, drawn, drew) closer.

6) Sushi is a (habitual, traditional, perpetual) Japanese food (consisting, containing, confer) of raw (meat, vegetables, fish).

7) Marco Polo was the (greatest, greeting, greater) of the medieval travellers, (pioneering, informing, introducing) Europeans to Central Asia and China through his detailed (adjourns, journals, journeys).

8) The city of Pompeii was (abolished, terminated, destroyed) when Mount Vesuvius (ejected, erupted, emitted) in the first (century, centaur, centres).

9) Attila was king of the Huns in 433, a group of (nominal, nomadic, nominee) people who (roamed, meandered, settled) Eastern Europe and were known for their (barber, barefoot, barbaric) practices.

10) Jupiter, the (filth, fifth, firth) planet from the Sun, is the (main, largest, greatest) planet in our (solar, solder, soler) system.

Cloze passages include various forms of text:
Historical • Biographical
General Knowledge • Literary Text Prose & Poetry

a. Historical

Exercise 2: 2 Select the correct words to complete the passage:

The 'Gunpowder Plot'

The 'Gunpowder Plot' was the name given to a **1)** ☐ treason / ☐ conspiracy / ☐ conquest

for blowing up King James I and the parliament on the 5th November 1605. The plotters **2)** ☐ leased / ☐ bestowed / ☐ imparted a cellar, situated

3) ☐ imminently / ☐ immediately / ☐ immobile beneath the House of Lords, in which Guy

Fawkes **4)** ☐ attired / ☐ idolised / ☐ arranged barrels of gunpowder, which he covered

over with firewood and coals to **5)** ☐ increase / ☐ decrease / ☐ endure the force of the

6) ☐ plot / ☐ plan / ☐ explosion . A slow match was prepared which would give him a quarter of an hour in which to **7)** ☐ escape ☐ seep ☐ thwart from the

explosion. However an **8)** ☐ anomalous ☐ anonymous ☐ unanimous letter revealing their

plans was sent to the **9)** ☐ evidences ☐ sources ☐ authorities and Fawkes was arrested

in the early hours of 5th November. He was **10)** ☐ exempted ☐ exhorted ☐ executed

alongside his conspirators opposite the Parliament House.

b. Biographical

Exercise 2: 3 Select the correct words to complete the passage:

Score

Florence Nightingale

From her earliest years Florence Nightingale's love of nature and

animals **1)** ☐ manifested ☐ accented ☐ sufficed itself. Her games, too, were

2) ☐ characters
    ☐ character
    ☐ characteristic
, for her great delight was to 3) ☐ remedy
                                   ☐ nurse
                                   ☐ medicine

and bandage her dolls. Her first living 4) ☐ patient
                                            ☐ patience
                                            ☐ patent
was a

shepherd's dog. From 5) ☐ cultivating
                        ☐ tending
                        ☐ supervising
animals she passed to

human beings, and wherever there was sorrow or suffering she was

sure to be 6) ☐ realised
              ☐ annoyed
              ☐ found
. In the year 1854, England was stirred

to its depths by the 7) ☐ retort
                        ☐ report
                        ☐ repent
of the sufferings of the sick and

wounded in the Crimea. To Miss Nightingale this 8) ☐ accrued
                                                   ☐ forfeited
                                                   ☐ proved

the trumpet-call of duty. She wrote to Sidney Herbert, secretary at

war, and 9) ☐ offered
            ☐ presented
            ☐ advanced
her services. She gave herself, body

and 10) ☐ being
        ☐ soul
        ☐ psyche
, to the work.

c. General Knowledge

Exercise 2: 4 Select the correct words to complete the passage:

April Fools' Day

April Fools' Day is the name given to the 1st of April, alluding to the custom of playing 1) ☐ trick / ☐ practical / ☐ funny jokes on friends on that day, or sending them on fools' errands. The 2) ☐ origin / ☐ cause / ☐ affect of this custom has been much 3) ☐ uncertain / ☐ queried / ☐ disputed , and many 4) ☐ luscious / ☐ ludicrous / ☐ lumbered solutions have been suggested. It has been 5) ☐ plausibly / ☐ potentially / ☐ genuine suggested that Europe 6) ☐ began / ☐ receive / ☐ derived its April-fooling from the French. They were the first nation to 7) ☐ adopt / ☐ clasp / ☐ envelop the reformed calendar in 1564, **8)** ☐ daunting ☐ debating ☐ decreeing that the year should begin with

the 1st of January. Thus New Year's gifts which has been the feature

of the 1st of April became **9)** ☐ incorporated ☐ associated ☐ aligned with the first day

of January, and those who **10)** ☐ disliked ☐ disapproving ☐ demeaned the change

became targets for those who amused themselves by sending mock presents on the 1st of April.

d. Literary Text Prose & Poetry

Exercise 2: 5 Select the correct words to complete the passage:
Little Women

"Christmas won't be Christmas without any **1)** ☐ presence ☐ pretence ☐ presents ,"

2) ☐ mumble ☐ grumbled ☐ tumbled Jo, lying on the rug.

"It's so dreadful to be **3)** ☐ poor ☐ meek ☐ humble !" sighed Meg, looking down at her 4) ☐ pristine / ☐ old / ☐ fowl dress.

"I don't think it's fair for some girls to have plenty of pretty things, and other girls nothing at all," added little Amy, with an 5) ☐ injury / ☐ inject / ☐ injured sniff.

"We've got Father and Mother, and each other," said Beth 6) ☐ pleased / ☐ sullen / ☐ contentedly from her 7) ☐ corner / ☐ spaces / ☐ plaice.

The four young faces on which the firelight shone 8) ☐ brightens / ☐ brightened / ☐ brighter at the cheerful words, but darkened again as Jo said sadly,—"We haven't got Father, and shall not have him for a long time." She didn't say 9) "☐ undeniable / ☐ certain / ☐ perhaps never," but each 10) ☐ inaudible / ☐ silently / ☐ loquaciously added it, thinking of Father far away, where the fighting was.

An extract from *Little Women* by Louisa May Alcott (1832-1888).

2. Multiple-choice Type 2

In the second type of **Multiple-choice** style question there are five alternatives for each missing word in the cloze passage.

Example:

Read the following cloze passage and identify the missing word from each multiple-choice option.

Puzzlewood

Puzzlewood is an 1) [A: expand] [B: city] [C: region] [D: area] [E: field] of woodland in the Forest of Dean in Gloucestershire. This place is 2) [A: extra] [B: general] [C: seldom] [D: rare] [E: often] used as a popular filming location. It is suggested that J R R Tolkien's Middle Earth was inspired 3) [A: of] [B: buy] [C: by] [D: for] [E: from] Puzzlewood as it has a unique atmosphere. There is a 4) [A: less] [B: lot] [C: much] [D: small] [E: some] of wild garlic in the vicinity, filling the air with its 5) [A: strong] [B: week] [C: weak] [D: bright] [E: loud] aroma.

1. Read the whole passage and try to establish what it is about, as this will provide clues for each missing word. This passage gives information on a place called Puzzlewood. The following approach applies to all five questions, but this explanation focuses on questions 1 and 2:

Puzzlewood is an 1) [expand|A] [city|B] [region|C] [area|D] [field|E] of woodland in the Forest of Dean in Gloucestershire. This place is 2) [extra|A] [general|B] [seldom|C] [rare|D] [often|E] used as a popular filming location.

2. Eliminate any words that do not fit grammatically.

   Puzzlewood is an **city/region/field** of woodland in the Forest of Dean in Gloucestershire. This place is **extra/general/rare** used as a popular filming location.

   Neither **city** nor **region** nor **field** work in question 1, as these need the prepostition 'a' before the question, not 'an'.

   Nor do **extra** or **general** or **rare** work in question 2 either, as the sentence requires an adverb in this position.

3. Check for any words that do not fit the meaning.

   Puzzlewood is an **expand** of woodland in the Forest of Dean in Gloucestershire. This place is **seldom** used as a popular filming location.

   expand does not work in question 1, as this is about an expanse of land.

   seldom does not work in question 2, as Puzzlewood is described as a 'popular filming location', implying it is used a lot.

4. Try the remaining words in the passage and see if they work.

   Puzzlewood is an **area** of woodland in the Forest of

Dean in Gloucestershire. This place is **often** used as a popular filming location.

Both of these words work in the passage.

area works because Puzzlewood is a space in the woodland.

often works because Puzzlewood is a popular location.

The answers are:

1. area 2. often

Using the same process the other questions will give the following answers: **3. by 4. lot 5. strong**

After each exercise has been completed and marked it is important to look up in a dictionary the meanings of the words that have been incorrectly selected. It is also crucial to take note of any grammatical, punctuation, syntactical or contextual errors that might have led to the wrong selection.

a. Historical

Exercise 2: 6   Select the correct words to complete the passage:

Maya Culture

Score

The Maya were an ancient people 1) [best] [unknown] [well] [lead] [known]
                                    A   B   C   D   E

for their pyramids, city construction and stone monuments.

2) [Those] [Them] [These] [They] [This] have fascinated archaeologists
     A   B   C   D   E

and historians since they were

3) | recovered | find | invented | discovered | hidden | . Excavations
       A   B   C   D   E

have 4) | closed | cracked | uncovered | concealed | opened | temples,
       A   B   C   D   E

palaces, pyramids, and many interesting archaeological remains.

The Maya were very 5) | religious | royal | discreet | ignorant | pompous |,
       A   B   C   D   E

worshipping various gods related to nature. The kings of the

Maya claimed to be related to these gods and were believed to be

mediators 6) | between | about | to | through | except | the gods and the
       A   B   C   D   E

Mayan people. The Maya also created a calendar

7) | methods | system | term | plan | month |, both to display 365 days
     A   B   C   D   E

and to indicate a long 5,126-year period, which ended on the 21st of

December 2012. It is unknown 8) | whine | where | who | why | while |
                                           A   B   C D   E

the Maya left their great cities to live in agricultural villages,

where the Spanish invaders conquered them in the 17th century.

Descendants of the Maya still live in Central America,

9) | which | and | at | while | with | the majority living in Guatemala.
      A   B   C   D   E

Tourists can 10) | visit | journey | travel | stay | find | the Tikal National
                  A   B   C   D   E

Park to see the ruins of the ancient city of Tikal, the capital of Maya.

b. Biographical

Exercise 2: 7

Select the correct words to complete the passage:

Score

Joseph Mallord William Turner

Joseph Mallord William Turner was 1) [birth A] [died B] [lost C] [found D] [born E] near Covent Garden, in London, in 1775. At 14 years old, he entered the Royal Academy of Arts as a child prodigy. He 2) [last A] [began B] [first C] [early D] [wanted E] exhibited his art at the Royal Academy in 1790. He began with watercolours, and 3) [than A] [then B] [there C] [that D] [thin E] moved on to oils, showing his first 4) [piece A] [art B] [sculpture C] [paint D] [peace E] in 1796. He was a prolific artist, leaving over 550 oil paintings, 2,000 watercolours and 30,000 artworks produced on paper. Turner had a 5) [good A] [great B] [grate C] [excellent D] [best E] interest in colour and he 6) [lost A] [convey B] [work C] [used D] [practise E] this in his landscapes and seascapes. He had 7) [two A] [few B] [one C] [three D] [couple E] daughters - Evelina and Georgiana. He is known 8) [apart A] [only B] [alone C] [simple D] [but E] as William Turner; his first two

© 2014 Stephen Curran

39

9) | brands | titles | names | signs | tag | are usually left out. He left most
      A   B   C   D   E

of his artwork to the nation. Since his death in 1851, aged 76, the

majority of his paintings have been displayed in national galleries.

Currently, these can be viewed at Tate Britain. Turner was

10) | solved | leave | died | buried | exhumed | in St Paul's Cathedral in
       A   B   C   D   E

London.

c. General Knowledge

Exercise 2: 8   Select the correct words to complete the passage:

Score

Sleeping Well

Sleep 1) | as | is | was | has | it | essential for a person's health and
            A   B   C   D   E

wellbeing. The amount of sleep a person needs depends on their age.

Babies sleep for 2) | less | more | during | up | through | to 15 hours per
                      A   B   C   D   E

day; children up 3) | as | at | to | too | two | the age
                      A   B   C   D   E

4) | on | if | to | of | off | 12 need up to 11 hours of sleep per day; and
     A   B   C   D   E

most adults need only eight hours per day. Sleep allows the brain to

rest, reset and problem-solve. Some people have a nap

5) | along | as well as | additionally | addition to | in addition | their
      A   B   C   D   E

nightly sleep. A nap can refresh someone and enable them to have

6) amount | much | less | enough | adequate energy to get on with
   A   B   C   D   E

the rest of their day. The 7) most | least | much | less | best effective
                              A   B   C   D   E

nap time is up to 30 minutes. Any longer will make the person feel

8) even | since | most | though | less more tired. Naps are traditionally
   A   B   C   D   E

taken in hot countries in the early afternoon. This is

9) regarded | title | name | known | called a siesta. A person usually
   A   B   C   D   E

yawns as a 10) symbolise | signs | signature | indicate | signal they
               A   B   C   D   E

are tired before going to sleep.

d. Literary Text

Exercise 2: 9 Select the correct words to complete the passage:

Gathering Leaves

Score

Spades take up leaves

No better than 1) spoons | bags | forks | gloves | mouse
                  A   B   C   D   E

And bags full of leaves

Are 2) colour | air | light | happy | heavy as balloons.
       A   B   C   D   E

I make a great 3) belief | noise | fall | rise | quiet
                  A   B   C   D   E

Of rustling all day

Like rabbit and deer

4) borrowing | running | chasing | eating | sleeping away.
   A   B   C   D   E

But the mountains I raise

Avoid my embrace,

Flowing over my arms

And into my face.

I may 5) store | drop | load | filled | pick and unload
         A   B   C   D   E

6) never | every | away | before | again and again
   A   B   C   D   E

Till I fill the whole shed,

And what have I then?

Next to nothing for weight,

And since they grew 7) full | better | colourful | duller | bright
                       A   B   C   D   E

From contact with earth,

8) shade | full | under | next | less to nothing for colour.
   A   B   C   D   E

Next to nothing to use,

But a crop is a crop,

And 9) who's | whose | who'd | who | who'll to say where
       A   B   C   D   E

The harvest shall 10) go | droop | clear | scoop | stop ?
                      A   B   C   D   E

An adaptation of *Gathering Leaves* by Robert Frost (1874-1953).

3. Word Bank

In **Word Bank** style questions there are a number of alternatives provided in a set of words at the top of the page. Words are chosen from this word bank to fill the spaces in the cloze passage.

Example: Choose the correct words from the word bank to fill each space in the cloze passage.

Charles Dickens

| acknowledged | English | fictional |
| novelist | unprecedented | |

Charles Dickens (1812–1870) was an 1) _____ writer and social critic. He created some of the world's most memorable 2) _____ characters and is generally regarded as the greatest 3) _____ of the Victorian period. During his life, his works enjoyed 4) _____ fame, and by the twentieth century many critics and scholars 5) _____ his literary genius. His novels and short stories continue to be widely popular.

1. Read the whole passage and try to establish what the passage is about, as this will provide clues for each missing word. This passage is a short biography on the life of the writer Charles Dickens.

2. Take each word in turn and try to establish its part of speech and meaning:
   - **acknowledged** is a verb in the past tense. It means to recognise, accept or admit something.
   - **unprecedented** is an adjective and means never done or known before.
   - **fictional** is an adjective and refers to literature or narrative that is imaginary or made up by the author.
   - **novelist** is a noun that means someone who writes novels or books of fiction.
   - **English** could be a noun or adjective. As a noun it could mean our language or nationality and as an adjective it could be describing something or someone as English.

3. Examine each cloze space and look for clues in the text that might help you identify the correct word from the word bank. Mark the words that have been used to avoid confusion and the possibility of repeating the use of a word:

- 'an _____ writer' – The use of the article **an** means that only specific words will fit. It must also be an adjective as it describes the writer. There are only three choices: **fictional** – does not work as it would have to be **a fictional** and not **an fictional**. **Unprecedented** is possible but **English** seems more likely as it comes at the beginning of the biographical note and introduces Dickens.
- 'most memorable _____ characters' – This must be an adjective as it describes the characters. Only two adjectives remain: **unprecedented** and **fictional**. Characters would not usually be described as never having happened before so **unprecedented** is not

correct. It must be **fictional** as Dickens wrote novels about imaginary characters.

- 'greatest _____ of the Victorian period' – This must be a noun as **greatest** is an adjective that describes the missing word. Only the noun **novelist** remains and this fits as Dickens was a great writer of the period.
- 'his works enjoyed _____ fame' – Only the adjective **unprecedented** is left and this fits. The works of Charles Dickens did achieve a fame that had not been known before during the Victorian period.
- 'critics and scholars _____ his literary genius' – The critics and scholars were doing something so look for a verb. The only possibility is **acknowledged**.

The passage would therefore read:

Charles Dickens

Charles Dickens (1812–1870) was an **English** writer and social critic. He created some of the world's most memorable **fictional** characters and is generally regarded as the greatest **novelist** of the Victorian period. During his life, his works enjoyed **unprecedented** fame, and by the twentieth century many critics and scholars **acknowledged** his literary genius. His novels and short stories continue to be widely popular.

After each exercise has been completed and marked it is important to look up the meanings of the words that have been incorrectly selected in a dictionary as an aid to learning. It is also crucial to take note of any grammatical, punctuation, syntactical or contextual errors that might have led to the wrong selection.

a. Historical

Exercise 2: 10 Choose the correct words from the word bank to complete the passage below:

Score

Gladiators

| combatants | trumpet | spectacle | desired | condemned |
| conquered | favour | wounded | wooden | entertain |

Gladiators were professional **1)** _____ who fought to the death to **2)** _____ audiences in Roman public shows. They were commonly drawn either from slaves or criminals **3)** _____ to death. The **4)** _____ began with a procession of the gladiators through the arena, after which the proceedings opened with a mock fight with **5)** _____ swords and javelins. The signal for real fighting was given by the sound of the **6)** _____ . When a gladiator was **7)** _____ , he lifted up his forefinger to implore the clemency of the people. If the spectators were in **8)** _____ of mercy, they waved their handkerchiefs; if they **9)** _____ the death of the **10)** _____ gladiator, they turned their thumbs downwards.

b. Biographical

Exercise 2: 11 Choose the correct words from the word bank to complete the passage below:

Jane Austen

| recognition | anonymously | author | marry | culture |
| uneventful | established | chiefly | except | retiring |

The English **1)** _____ Jane Austen, (1775-1817), was born on the 16th of December 1775 at the parsonage of Steventon, in Hampshire. The life of no woman of genius could have been more **2)** _____ than Miss Austen's. She did not **3)** _____ , and she never left home **4)** _____ on short visits, **5)** _____ to Bath. Her best-known, if not her best work, *Pride and Prejudice*, was also her first. All her works were published **6)** _____ , agreeably to their author's **7)** _____ disposition. **8)** _____ came to Miss Austen slowly. It was not until quite recent times that to read her became a necessity of **9)** _____ . But she is now firmly **10)** _____ as an English classic.

c. General Knowledge

Exercise 2: 12 Choose the correct words from the word bank to complete the passage below:

Avalanches

| downward | mingled | sometimes | rushes | everything |
| accumulate | thunder | compacted | cause | effect |

An avalanche is a mass of snow and ice 1) _____ with earth and stones, which 2) _____ down a mountain side, carrying 3) _____ before it. A mass of snow may 4) _____ upon a steep slope and become 5) _____ into ice by pressure, or remain loosely aggregated. When the foundation gives way, owing to the loosening effect of spring rains or from any other 6) _____ , the whole mass slides 7) _____ slowly in the form of glaciers, or suddenly in avalanches. A very small cause will 8) _____ set a mass of overloaded snow in motion. 9) _____ or even a loud shout is said to produce this 10) _____ when the mass is just poised.

d. Literary Text Prose & Poetry

Exercise 2: 13 Choose the correct words from the word bank to complete the passage below:

 Score

Sing, Little Birdie!

| topmost | tear | forever | livelong | only |
| hide | die | sing | ring | spreadst |

Sing, little birdie, 1) _____

On 2) _____ branches high!

And when thou 3) _____ thy airy wing,

Let not the sweet notes 4) _____ ,

But longer, louder be,

Until the echoes 5) _____

That 6) _____ away where none may see,

But 7) _____ hear them sing.

Methinks that I could stay

8) _____ with thee here,

And list thy strain the 9) _____ day,

Forgetting sorrow's 10) _____ .

By Watie W Swanzy (published in 1889).

3. Missing Letters

In **Missing Letters** style questions the cloze passage has a number of words where letters are absent. Some of the key letters are provided to assist in the completion of the words.

Consonants and Vowels

It can be helpful to split up consonants and vowels when trying out various letters in spaces. Working through the alphabet is useful, as this does not take long.
Remember that:

- There are 21 consonants and some are rarely used, such as **q**, **x** and **z**. This narrows it down to 18 regularly used consonants.

- There are five vowels and **u** is used less frequently, narrowing it down to four regularly used vowels.

Letter Combinations

When attempting missing letters questions remember that there are some rules that can help you identify missing letters:

- Certain consonants cannot be next to each other, e.g. **p** cannot be followed by **q** to make **pq**.

- Some same vowels cannot be next to each other, e.g. **u** cannot follow **u** to make **uu**.

- Some letters always go together, e.g. **qu**.

- Some vowels often go together, e.g. **ee**, **ea**, **ia**, etc.

- Some consonants often join together to form a different sound, e.g. **th** or **ph**.

- Most words begin with a consonant and end with a consonant, e.g. **boat**.

- A small number of words begin and end with a vowel, e.g. **era**.

Example:

> Fill in the missing letters to complete the passage below.
>
> **Song**
>
> Two doves upon the selfsame 1) | b | | | n | | | ,
> Two lilies on a 2) | | i | | g | | e | stem,
> Two 3) | | u | | e | | f | | i | | s | upon one flower:--
> Oh happy they who look on them.
>
> Who look upon them hand in hand
> Flushed in the rosy 4) | s | | | m | | | light;
> Who look upon them hand in hand
> And never give a thought to 5) | n | | | h | | .
>
> By Christina Rossetti (1830-1894).

1. Read the poem carefully and try and establish what it is about. This poem is about someone observing and commenting on the beauty of nature.

2. Look for any rhyming words at the end of a line as this may enable you to identify one word straight away. Every second and fourth line rhymes in each stanza. This means the last word of line four of stanza two must rhyme with the last word of line two in the same stanza. Hence, the word in question 5) | n | | | h | | must rhyme with **light**. If we focus on the first letter **n** and think of what rhymes with **light**, **night** is the only possibility.

3. Now look at the context of each other word and look for clues in the parts of speech:

- 'Two doves upon the selfsame `b _ _ n _ _`' - this word must be a noun and the context is helpful. What would two birds sit upon that begins with **b**? It must be a **branch**.
- 'Two lilies on a `_ i _ g _ e` stem' – this word must be an adjective as it describes the **stem**. What could two lilies be on that is linked to **stem**? Not many words end in `g _ e` so the missing letter is probably an **l**. We now have `_ i _ g l e` and if we go through the consonants of the alphabet to find the first letter, we will eventually come to **s** meaning the word must be **single**.
- 'Two `_ u _ e _ f _ i _ s` upon one flower' – this word must a be a noun. What would settle upon one flower? It must be an insect of some sort. Again, if we go through the consonants of the alphabet to find the first letter we will almost immediately come to **b**. The word is obviously **butterflies**.
- 'Flushed in the rosy `s _ _ m _ _` light' – this must be an adjective that describes light. The first letter is a very strong clue. If we try the five vowels in the next missing space we will come to **u**. This should be enough of a clue to identify the word as **summer**.

4. Read the poem through to check all the missing letters that have been filled in make sensible words that fit the context. We can now identify the poem as *Song* by Christina Rossetti.

Song
Two doves upon the selfsame **branch**,

Two lilies on a **single** stem,
Two **butterflies** upon one flower:--
Oh happy they who look on them.

Who look upon them hand in hand
Flushed in the rosy **summer** light;
Who look upon them hand in hand
And never give a thought to **night**.

By Christina Rossetti (1830-1894).

The correct words are:
       1) branch 2) single 3) butterflies
                4) summer 5) night

After each exercise has been completed and marked it is important to look up the spellings and meanings of any words that were either missed out or incorrectly spelt. It is also crucial to take note of any grammatical, punctuation, syntactical and contextual errors that might have led to these mistakes.

a. Historical

Exercise 2: 14 Fill in the missing letters to complete the passage below:

Score

Hieroglyphics

Hieroglyphics is the term used to describe the

1) | c | h | | r | | | t | e | | s | of the ancient Egyptian

2) | l | | n | g | | | | | . Although

3) [|t|t| | |p|t|] were made to read hieroglyphs as far back as the 17th 4) [c| | |t| | |y], no promise of success appeared until the 5) [|i|s|c| |v| | |y] of the Rosetta Stone in 1709. The Rosetta Stone is a stone tablet 6) [i|n|s| | |b| |d] in three languages, in hieroglyphic, Demotic (everyday Egyptian) and Ancient Greek. The discovery of the Rosetta Stone placed the key to the hieroglyphics within Western reach, and the stone was finally 7) [|r| | |s|l|a| |e|d] in the 1820's by Jean-François Champollion, 8) [e|n| |b|l| | |] people to read other Ancient Egyptian 9) [w| | |t| |n|g|] and 10) [c| | |s| |q| |e|n|t|] learn about Ancient Egyptian life.

b. Biographical

Exercise 2: 15 Fill in the missing letters to complete the passage below:

Score

Spencer Perceval

Spencer Perceval is the only British 1) | P | | | | e | Minister to

have been assassinated. He was 2) | e | d | | a | | | at

Trinity College, Cambridge, and studied law at Lincoln's Inn in 1786.

As a professional 3) | l | | w | | | he held the senior

4) | p | o | | | i | o | | s | of Solicitor General and Attorney

General. Perceval was Prime Minister of 5) | | n | g | | | d |

for only three years when he was shot by a man named John

Bellingham in the lobby of the House of 6) | C | | | m | | n | s |

on the 11th of May 1812. Bellingham was a bankrupt

7) | | u | s | i | | | | m | | n | with a grievance, who had

8) [|s|u|c| | | | |f|u| |l|] applied to him for compensation. Bellingham was 9) [t| | | |d] , where 10) [e|v| | | |n|c|] was presented that he was insane, but he was found guilty and hanged for his murder.

c. General Knowledge

Exercise 2: 16 Fill in the missing letters to complete the passage below:

Score

Budapest

Budapest is the 1) [c| |p| | | |l] and largest town of the 2) [E|u| | |p| | |n] country Hungary. The city is 3) [|i|t| |a| | |d] on both banks of the Danube River, and is formed of the former 4) [| |o|w| | |s] of Buda on the western bank, and of Pest on the 5) [| | | |t|e|r|n] bank, which were all incorporated into one municipality in 1872. Situated nearly in the **6)** c _ _ t r _ of Hungary, the

7) _ m p o _ i _ g size of the Danube, and the

8) s h _ _ p contrast of the two banks, place Budapest among

the most finely located of the larger towns of Europe. Buda, with its

royal palace, the various ministries, and other

9) g _ v _ r _ m _ _ t offices, is the official centre,

while Pest is the **10)** c _ m _ _ _ c i _ l and

industrial part.

d. Literary Text Prose & Poetry

Exercise 2: 17 Fill in the missing letters to complete the passage below:

Score

The Secret Garden

She **1)** l _ _ _ e d at the key quite a long time. She

2) _ u r n _ _ it over and over, and thought about it.

As I have said before, she was not a child who had been trained to ask 3) **permission** or consult her 4) **elders** about things. All she thought 5) **about** the key was that if it was the key to the closed garden, and she could find out 6) **where** the door was, she could 7) **perhaps** open it and see what was 8) **inside** the walls, and what had 9) **happened** to the old rose-trees. It was 10) **because** it had been shut up so long that she wanted to see it.

An extract from *The Secret Garden* by Frances Hodgson Burnett (1849-1924).

Chapter Three
REVISION
1. Classification

Exercise 3: 1   Underline the odd one out:

1) amber, gold, grape, mustard, saffron

2) antiseptic, disinfected, sterile, antibacterial, infected

Underline the word which is a synonym of the word in bold:

3) **PETULANT**   patient   fractious   naughty   chaotic   dirty

Complete the word on the right by filling in the missing letters. It is a synonym of the word on the left.

4) **callous** | _ | r | u | _ | l |

5) **impractical** | f | _ | i | v | _ | l | o | _ | s |

Underline the word which is an antonym of the word in bold:

6) **WARY**   suspicious   frugal   signal   certain   obscure

Complete the word on the right by filling in the missing letters. It is an antonym of the word on the left:

7) **meticulous** | c | _ | r | _ | l | _ | _ | s |

8) **insolent** | _ | r | _ | s | p | e | _ | t | _ | u | l |

Underline the one word which will link the two pairs of bracketed words:

9) (healthy, complete)   sturdy sound normal
   (noise, note)   melody robust

10) (outright, absolute) articulate sheer blurt
    (express, proclaim)   utter chime

Score

2. Cloze

Exercise 3: 2   Select the correct words to complete the passages:

Christopher Columbus

Score

Christopher Columbus was an Italian explorer who

1) ☐ sales
   ☐ journey   across the Atlantic Ocean into the unknown. He
   ☐ voyaged

was attempting to find a new western sea route in 2) ☐ order
                                                    ☐ able   to
                                                    ☐ so

                            ☐ left
trade with Asia and 3)   ☐ went   sail on the 3rd of August 1492.
                            ☐ set

Columbus and his crew spent 36 days at sea until they found

    ☐ land   ☐ settled
4) ☐ island , eventually 5) ☐ arriving   on the shores of
    ☐ sea   ☐ rest

America.

Frankenstein

During this short voyage I saw the 6) [stormy / lighting / thunder / lightning / lightening] (A/B/C/D/E) flashing on the summit of Mont Blanc in the most beautiful way. The storm appeared to approach 7) [slow / rapidly / quick / seldom / often] (A/B/C/D/E), and, on landing, I 8) [clambers / descended / hiked / climb / ascended] (A/B/C/D/E) a low hill, so that I could observe its progress. It advanced; the sky clouded 9) [on / over / above / through / in] (A/B/C/D/E), and I soon felt the rain coming slowly in large drops, but 10) [that / them / their / its / it's] (A/B/C/D/E) violence quickly became more intense.

An adapted extract from *Frankenstein* by Mary Shelley (1797-1851).

Exercise 3: 3

Choose the correct words from the word bank to complete the passage below:

Archery

| combat | sport | propel | traced | target |

The sport of archery involves using a bow to 1) _____ arrows towards a 2) _____. Historically, the skill was used predominantly for hunting and **3)** _____ but in the modern world it is mainly a competitive **4)** _____. The first use of a bow can be **5)** _____ back to over 10,000 years ago.

Fill in the missing letters to complete the passage below.

Dictionaries

A dictionary is a book or an electronic **6)** | r | | s | o | | | c | e |

that contains a collection of **7)** | w | | | d | s | in one or more

specific languages. The words are **8)** | t | y | | i | | | l | y |

arranged in **9)** | | l | p | | a | b | | t | i | c | | l | order and

each entry contains information regarding its definition,

10) | p | r | o | n | | | c | i | | t | i | | n | , origin and

usage.

Score

Answers

11+ English Year 5-7
Workbook 1

Chapter One
Classification

Exercise 1: 1
1) visor
2) hurricane
3) Istanbul
4) cousin
5) gazelle
6) dragonfly
7) veal
8) Europe
9) group
10) popular

Exercise 1: 2
1) demon
2) tight
3) mound
4) trail
5) game
6) draw
7) abridge
8) gangue
9) later
10) yummy

Exercise 1: 3
1) gloomy
2) vigorous
3) ancient
4) mediocre
5) invalid
6) abyss
7) triumph
8) curtail
9) provoke
10) dissuade

Exercise 1: 4
1) repose
2) baulk
3) lagoon
4) squander
5) moccasins
6) hostile
7) anemone
8) abscess
9) riser
10) ire

Exercise 1: 5
1) valiant
2) amusing
3) emotional
4) location
5) smart
6) cruel
7) struggle
8) bland
9) break
10) article

Exercise 1: 6
1) poem
2) delete
3) vulgar
4) exclusive
5) manage
6) badger
7) scoundrel
8) subtitle
9) unattached
10) convention

Exercise 1: 7
1) even
2) ignite
3) discard
4) confine
5) envisage
6) mix
7) comprehension
8) slander
9) error
10) fatherly

Exercise 1: 8
1) distanced
2) experienced
3) courteous
4) unconfirmed
5) calm
6) present
7) dwindle
8) lethargy
9) wicked
10) placid

Exercise 1: 9
1) fail
2) hopeful
3) untruthful
4) microscopic
5) attractive
6) remain
7) damage
8) peaceful
9) dishonesty
10) reprimand

Exercise 1: 10
1) robust
2) stagnant
3) tender
4) elegant
5) surge
6) polluted
7) connect
8) divide
9) lax
10) confront

Exercise 1: 11
1) beat
2) fine
3) lie
4) light
5) mean
6) trunk
7) well
8) lead
9) wind
10) row

Exercise 1: 12
1) wound 2) desert
3) pound 4) content
5) band   6) ground
7) check 8) bear
9) rare   10) fan

Exercise 1: 13
1) refrain 2) bow
3) bank   4) bark
5) bait   6) desolate
7) block   8) bore
9) board   10) root

Chapter Two
Cloze

Exercise 2: 1
1) magician, appear, thin
2) art, needles, cloth
3) delayed, due, track
4) highest, situated, dormant
5) lost, frostbite, drew
6) traditional, consisting, fish
7) greatest, introducing, journals
8) destroyed, erupted, century
9) nomadic, roamed, barbaric
10) fifth, largest, solar

11+ English Year 5-7
Workbook 1

Answers

Exercise 2: 2
1) conspiracy
2) leased
3) immediately
4) arranged
5) increase
6) explosion
7) escape
8) anonymous
9) authorities
10) executed

Exercise 2: 3
1) manifested
2) characteristic
3) nurse
4) patient
5) tending
6) found
7) report
8) proved
9) offered
10) soul

Exercise 2: 4
1) practical
2) origin
3) disputed
4) ludicrous
5) plausibly
6) derived
7) adopt
8) decreeing
9) associated
10) disliked

Exercise 2: 5
1) presents
2) grumbled
3) poor
4) old
5) injured
6) contentedly
7) corner
8) brightened
9) perhaps
10) silently

Exercise 2: 6
1) known
2) These
3) discovered
4) uncovered
5) religious
6) between
7) system
8) why
9) with
10) visit

Exercise 2: 7
1) born
2) first
3) then
4) piece
5) great
6) used
7) two
8) only
9) names
10) buried

Exercise 2: 8
1) is
2) up
3) to
4) of
5) as well as
6) enough
7) most
8) even
9) called
10) signal

Exercise 2: 9
1) spoons
2) light
3) noise
4) running
5) load
6) again
7) duller
8) next
9) who's
10) stop

Exercise 2: 10
1) combatants
2) entertain
3) condemned
4) spectacle
5) wooden
6) trumpet
7) wounded
8) favour
9) desired
10) conquered

Exercise 2: 11
1) author
2) uneventful
3) marry
4) except
5) chiefly
6) anonymously
7) retiring
8) recognition
9) culture
10) established

Exercise 2: 12
1) mingled
2) rushes
3) everything
4) accumulate
5) compacted
6) cause
7) downward
8) sometimes
9) thunder
10) effect

Exercise 2: 13
1) sing
2) topmost
3) spreadst
4) die
5) ring
6) hide
7) only
8) forever
9) livelong
10) tear

Exercise 2: 14
1) characters
2) language
3) attempts
4) century
5) discovery
6) inscribed
7) translated
8) enabling
9) writings
10) consequently

Exercise 2: 15
1) Prime
2) educated
3) lawyer
4) positions
5) England
6) Commons
7) businessman
8) unsuccessfully
9) tried
10) evidence

Answers

11+ English Year 5-7
Workbook 1

Exercise 2: 16
1) capital
2) European
3) situated
4) towns
5) eastern
6) centre
7) imposing
8) sharp
9) government
10) commercial

Exercise 2: 17
1) looked
2) turned
3) permission
4) elders
5) about
6) where
7) perhaps
8) inside
9) happened
10) because

Chapter Three
Revision
Exercise 3: 1
1) grape
2) infected
3) fractious
4) cruel
5) frivolous
6) certain
7) careless
8) respectful
9) sound
10) utter

Exercise 3: 2
1) voyaged
2) order
3) set
4) land
5) arriving
6) lightning
7) rapidly
8) ascended
9) over
10) its

Exercise 3: 3
1) propel
2) target
3) combat
4) sport
5) traced
6) resource
7) words
8) typically
9) alphabetical
10) pronunciation

PROGRESS CHARTS

Shade in your score for each exercise on the graph. Add up for your total score.

1. CLASSIFICATION

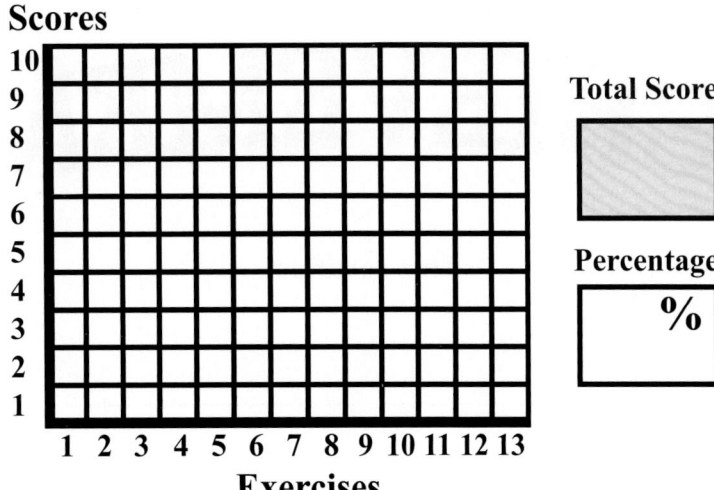

2. CLOZE

3. REVISION

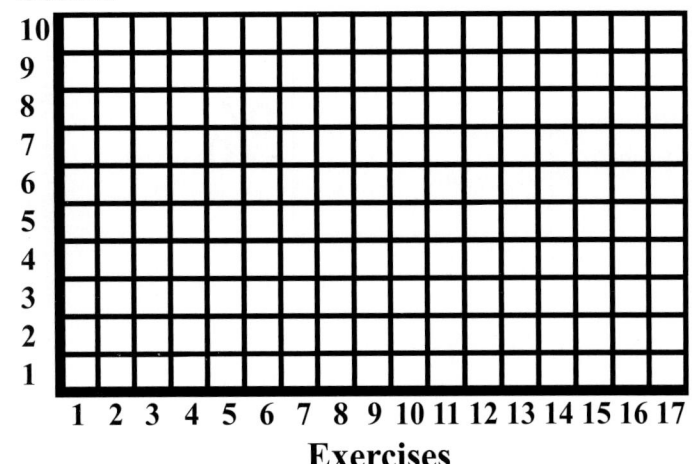

Add up the percentages and divide by 3

Overall Percentage   %

CERTIFICATE OF
ACHIEVEMENT

This certifies

_____

has successfully completed

11+ English
Year 5–7
WORKBOOK 1

Overall percentage score achieved ☐ %

Comment _____

_____

Signed _____
(teacher/parent/guardian)

Date _____